GO TELL THE CHILDREN

Sharon P. Carson

DEDICATION

To my grandchildren and great grand children, present and future
To aunt Liz for her inspiration

The greatness of our ancestors
Can never die you see
It lies too deep within the seeds
Of every apple from the tree

(Excerpted from the poem "Stolen Apples" Sharon P. Carson)

Author's Notes

"Go Tell The Children" is a transformative pictorial stroll through highlights in Black History. The book was not written to denigrate the Black youths who wear their pants sagged, to purposely show off their underwear, it was written to uplift them.

The pictorial cover of the book showing two Black youths wearing sagging pants is an effort by the author to awaken a youthful curiosity that may encourage further exploration of the book itself.

The author is not a historian neither is the book intended to be a textbook or a chronology of Black history. The book is not gendered specific, it was written for both males and females, for those who wear their pants sagging and for those who hopefully never will.

The book allows the reader to follow the transitioning of the two young men pictured on the cover of the book to the end of the book as they stroll through pages of Black history highlights of struggle, strength and great accomplishments, including the election of the first Black president of the United States of America.

The author hopes that the book will not just be an impetus for the pulling up of young men's pants across the nation, but will have the larger impact of the pulling up of one's self through education whereby they can show the nation their best side and not their backside.

GO TELL THE CHILDREN

To take pride in their blackness

And the heritage of their race

The United States Postal Service - through its Black Heritage stamp series, pays tribute to African American individuals and accomplishments that have transformed the nation

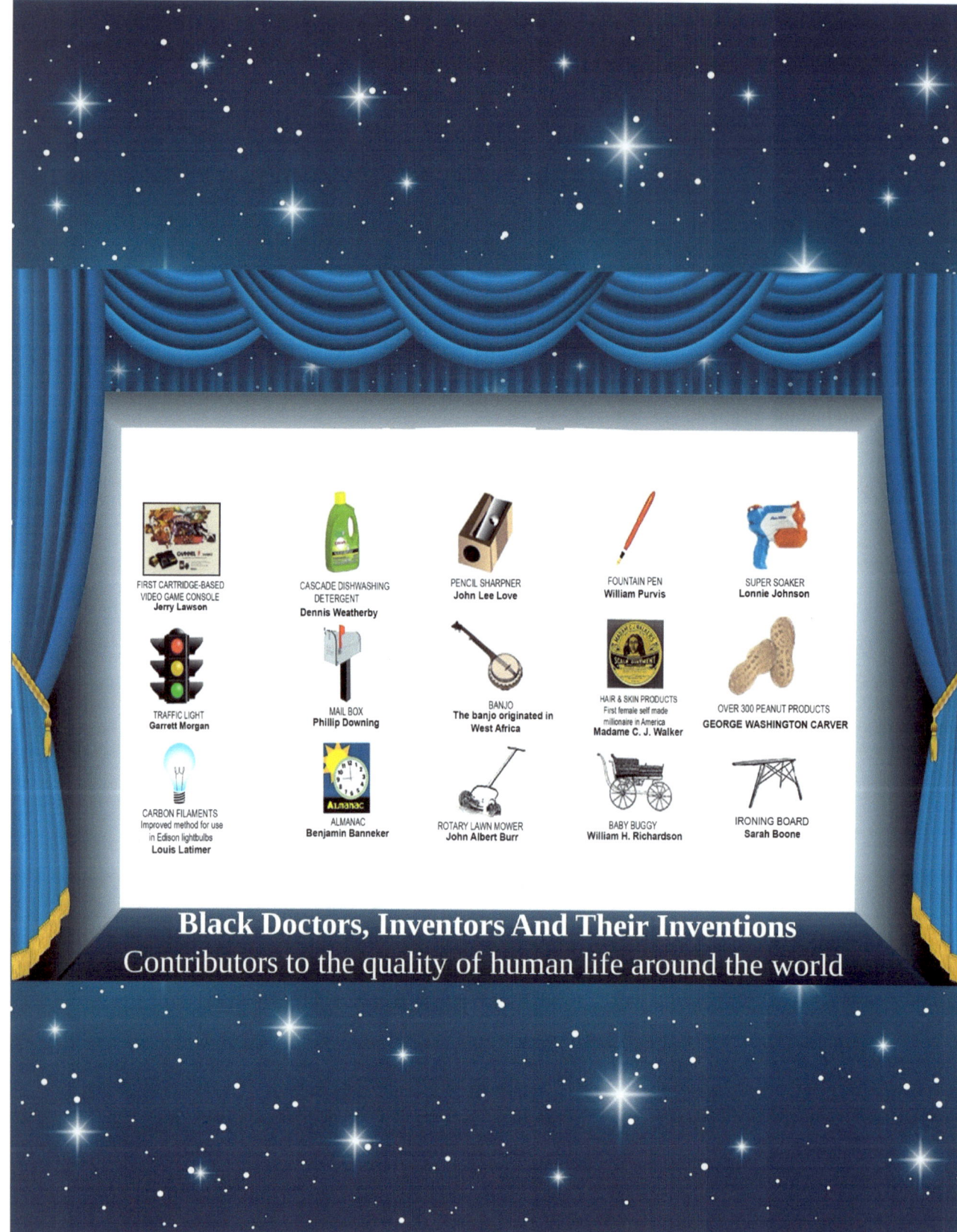

Which shines like stars
Despite the obstacles it faced

VENUS WILLIAMS - Professional Tennis Player
Became the first African American woman to be ranked #1 in the world
SERENA WILLIAMS - Professional Tennis Player
Won 23 Grand Slam singles titles. The all-time winner of women's Grand Slam titles in the Open Era

USAIN BOLT- Sprinter
Nickname "Lightning Bolt" - Widely considered to be the greatest sprinter of all time with nine Olympic gold medals.

DR. MAE JEMISON - Astronaut, Engineer, Physician
The first African-American woman to travel in space. She flew on space shuttle "Endeavour" in September of 1992

To embrace their blackness
And never from it run

To study their great heritage
Both daughters and sons

Tell them that Black History
Is as old as earth's first man

All of earth's population
Evolved from the African

Tell them about the pyramids
Built with strong black minds and hands

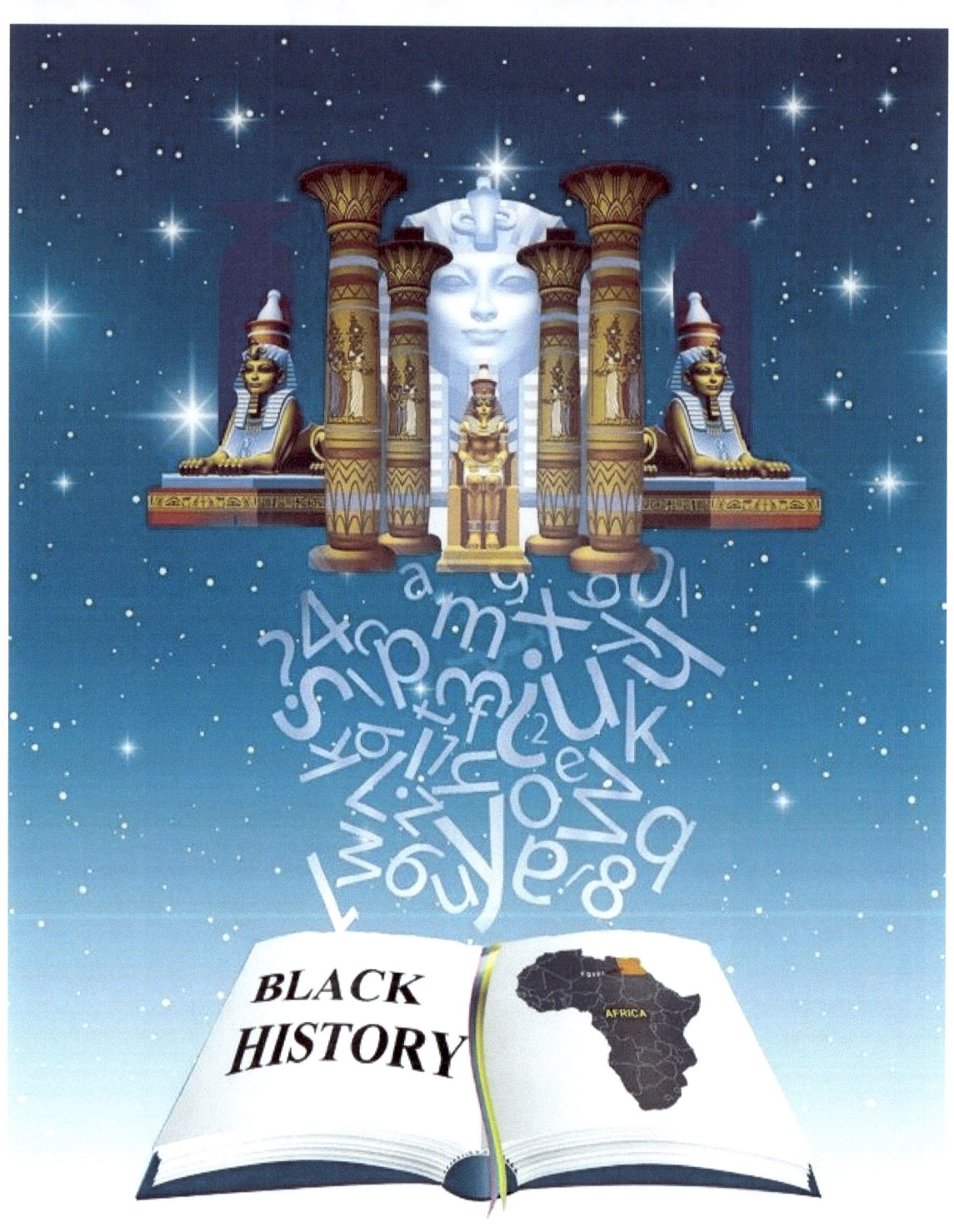

Tell them how our ancestors
Were taken from their African lands

UNITED STATES SLAVE TRADE,
1830.

Tell them of our enslavement
For over four hundred years

Picking Cotton on a Georgia Plantation

But tell them we too fought for freedom
With blood, sweat and tears

Tell them about the document
That brought slavery to an end

But tell them how we soon found out
New struggles would just begin

Tell them that our struggles
Have now become our strength
And the world has taken note

We pressed on to demand our equal rights
Among them the right to vote

Tell them how through the ballot
We elected many of African decent

THE FIRST BLACK SENATORS & REPRESENTATIVES
In the 41st & 42nd Congress of the Unites Stares

Tell them how we elected
Our first Black president

Senator Barack Hussein Obama became the 44th president of the United States of America on November 4, 2008. President Obama became the first African American to be elected to that office and served two terms as president

Michelle Obama - First lady of the United States of America

Tell them how through non-violence
We won our biggest fights

The March on Washington for Jobs and Freedom held on August 28, 1963 in Washington, D.C., was to that point the largest public protest in United States history.

As preached by Dr. Martin Luther King Jr.
A champion of civil rights

**Tell them how long we walked
Rather than sit at the back of the bus**

Rosa Parks, an African American woman, was arrested on December 1, 1955 for disobeying an Alabama law requiring Black passengers to sit at the back of the bus and give up their seats to white passengers when the bus was full. Her arrest sparked a 381 day boycott of the Montgomery bus system. Since many African Americans did not have cars they had to walk or carpool. The boycott lead to a 1956 Supreme Court decision banning segregation on public transportation.

Tell them how long we marched
So schools would open up to us

Tell them now the door is open
To all they choose to do

And will open even wider
As each one passes through

Tell them that the victory is theirs
When they equip themselves to win

But the war is not won
With a bullet and a gun
But with a book
A piece of paper and a pen

Contact Information

Sharon P. Carson

P. O. Box 437155
Chicago, IL. 60643
773-568-2274

Email: sharoncarsonbooks@gmail.com

Copyright 2017

All rights reserved. No part of this book may be reprinted or reproduced or utilized in any form or by any electronic, computerized, mechanical or other means, now known of hereafter invented, including photocopying and recording, or in any information storage or retrieval system, without permission in writing from Sharon P. Carson, Publisher.

ISBN: 978-0-9830751-9-6

Books by Sharon P. *Carson*
www.sharoncarsonbooks.com

ACT LIKE A LADY- THINK LIKE A MAN

YOU ARE MORE THAN "*MEATS"* THE EYE

SPIRIT TO SPIRIT

SOUL SONGS

HASHTAG #GOD

WHAT EVERY HOME APPRAISER KNOWS & EVERY HOMEOWNER SHOULD

HOW TO BECOME A REAL ESTATE APPRAISER